THE BLESSINGS OF LOVE

The Blessings of Love

MOTHER TERESA

SELECTED AND EDITED BY
NANCY SABBAG

CHARIS

SERVANT PUBLICATIONS
ANN ARBOR, MICHIGAN

Charis Books is an imprint of Servant Publications especially designed to serve Roman Catholics.

Published by Servant Publications, P.O. Box 8617, Ann Arbor, Michigan 48107

Material for this book was excerpted from the following Servant publications: *Heart of Joy,* © 1987; *Jesus, the Word to Be Spoken,* © 1986; *One Heart Full of Love,* © 1988; *Total Surrender,* © 1985. All rights reserved.

Cover design: Diane Bareis
Cover photo, landscape: Dennis Frates
Cover photo, Mother Teresa: Bettmann

03 04 05 06 14 13 12 11

Printed in the United States of America
ISBN 0-89283-975-9

LIBRARY OF CONGRESS CATALOGING-IN-PUBLICATION DATA

Teresa, Mother
    The blessings of love / Mother Teresa ; selected and edited by Nancy Sabbag.
      p.   cm.
    ISBN 0-89283-975-9
    1. Christian life—Catholic authors—Quotations, maxims, etc.   I. Sabbag, Nancy.   II. Title
BX2350.2.T465   1996
248.8'82—dc20   96-2360
                                                                              CIP

꒳

"We all long for heaven where God is, but we have it in our power to be in heaven with Him right now—to be happy with Him at this very moment. Being happy with Him now means loving like He loves, helping like He helps, giving as He gives, serving as He serves, rescuing as He rescues, being with Him twenty-four hours a day—touching Him in His distressing disguise."

Mother Teresa
Total Surrender

CONTENTS

⁊

Experiencing the Blessings of Love

Extending the Blessings of Love

Becoming a Blessing of Love

Experiencing the Blessings of Love

God's Love for Us

"God so loved the world that He gave His only Son." God still loves the world, and today He continues to give Jesus to the world through you and me....Each of us, in his own way, must be the Father's love and compassion toward the world.

"In Him we live and move and have our being." Consider that you are in God, surrounded and encompassed by God, swimming in God.

*I*n heaven everything was beautiful—yet, what attracted Jesus to the earth? The Son of God wanted to feel what it meant to be a human being; to be locked up for nine months, so dependent on a mother. That is why we say, "He, being rich, became poor."

*B*eing God, Jesus became like us in every way except sin. And He proclaimed clearly that He had come to bring good news. That good news was God's peace to all men of good will. That peace is something which is fundamental to the satisfaction of our most basic desires. It is a peace of the heart.

As if it were not enough—as if it were not enough to have become man—Jesus died on the cross to show us His great love. He died for you and for me.

*H*ow did Jesus love us? He became living bread that you and I might eat, that we might live. He became so small and so weak in order to meet our hunger for God.

*T*here is no limit to God's love. It is without measure, and its depth cannot be sounded. This is shown by His living and dying among us. Now turn the same picture around. There must be no limit to the love that prompts us to give ourselves to God, to be the victim of His unwanted love, that is, the love of God that has not been accepted by men.

God loves us with a tender love. That is all that Jesus came to teach us, the tender love of God. "I have called you by name, you are Mine."

Remember that when your heart feels restless, when your heart feels hurt, when your heart feels like breaking—then remember, "I am precious to Him. He loves me. He has called me by my name. I am His. He loves me. God loves me." And to prove that love He died on the cross.

*P*rovidence always comes to our help. When the need is immediate, the intervention of providence is also immediate. It is not always a matter of huge amounts, but of what is needed at a given moment.

"*B*e still and know that I am God." God requires us to be silent to discover Him. In the silence of the heart, He speaks to us.

I believe each time we say the Our Father, God looks at His hands, where He has carved us—"I have carved you on the palm of My hand"—He looks at His hands, and He sees us there. How wonderful the tenderness and love of the great God!

Our Significance to God

Look at the cross and you will know what one soul means to Jesus.

"You have not chosen Me, but I have chosen you." Jesus has chosen us for Himself. We belong to Him. Let us be so convinced of this belonging that we allow nothing, however small, to separate us from His love.

God loves me. I'm not here just to fill a place....He has chosen me for a purpose. I know it. He will fulfill it if I don't put an obstacle in His way. He will not force me. God could have forced Our Lady. Jesus could have come "just like that."… But God wanted Mary to say yes. It is the same with us. God doesn't force us, but He wants us to say yes.

We must know that we have been created for greater things, not just to be a number in the world, not just to go for diplomas and degrees, this work and that work. We have been created in order to love and to be loved.

No one spoils us as much as God Himself. See the wonderful gifts He has given us freely?...You can all see—if God were to take money for your sight what would happen? Continually we are breathing and living on oxygen we did not pay for.

Our Love for God

Don't allow anything to interfere with your love for Jesus. You belong to Him. *Nothing can separate you from Him* (Rom 8:38-39). That one sentence is important to remember.

A certain priest loved the Chinese and wanted to do something for them. He became so involved in the work that it seemed that even his eyes became slanted, like the Chinese. If I live constantly in the company of Jesus, I will look like Him and do as He did.

*C*hrist wants to offer us the means of putting our love for Him into action. He becomes hungry, not only for bread but for love. He becomes naked, not only for a piece of clothing but for love that understands, for human dignity. He becomes dispossessed, not only for a place of shelter but for the sincere and deep love for one another.

We do not need to carry out grand things in order to show great love for God and for our neighbor. It is the intensity of love we put into our gestures that makes them into something beautiful for God.

There is such a beautiful thing in India—the red dot on the forehead. The meaning for the Hindu is that his whole thought and attention, everything, must be concentrated on God. For the married woman it is the same. The red marking along the part in her hair means that all her thoughts are for her husband. We, too, must be fully for Jesus, giving Him that undivided love.

*T*he simplest way of becoming [Jesus'] light is by being kind and loving, thoughtful, and sincere with each other: "By this they will know that you are My disciples."

C hrist said, "I was hungry and you gave me food." He was hungry not only for bread but for the understanding love of being loved, of being known, of being someone to someone.

*T*here is a story of a little robin. He saw Jesus on the cross, saw the crown of thorns. The bird flew around and around until he found a way to remove a thorn—and in removing the thorn, it struck him. Each one of us should be that bird.

Zeal for souls is the effect and the proof of true love for God. If we really love God, we cannot but be consumed with the desire of saving souls, the greatest and dearest interest of Jesus.

Why must we give ourselves fully to God? Because God has given Himself to us. If God, who owes nothing to us, is ready to impart to us no less than Himself, shall we answer with just a fraction of ourselves?

Our Purpose in God

All of us have been given the opportunity to be completely possessed by Jesus. The work He has entrusted to you and me is nothing more than putting our love for Him into action. What you do I cannot do. What I do you cannot do. But together you and I can do something beautiful for God.

God has created us for great things: to love and offer love, to experience tenderness toward others, as He did, and to know how to offer Jesus to others. People are not hungry for us; they are hungry for God.

The work we do is nothing more than a means of transforming our love for Christ into something concrete.

God will not ask [us] how many books we have read; how many miracles we have worked; but He will ask [us] if we have done our best, for the love of Him.

We are at [Jesus'] disposal. If He wants you to be sick in bed, if He wants you to proclaim His work in the street, if He wants you to clean the toilets all day, that's all right, everything is all right. We must say, "I belong to You. You can do whatever You like." And this...is our strength, and this is the joy of the Lord.

*E*ach time anyone comes into contact with us, they must become different and better people because of having met us. We must radiate God's love.

Our ideal is no one but Jesus. We must think as He thinks, love as He loves, wish as He wishes; we must permit Him to use us to the full.

You may be exhausted with work,
even kill yourself,
but unless your work is
interwoven with love,
it is useless.

*T*he important thing is not how much we accomplish, but how much love we put into our deeds every day. That is the measure of our love for God.

Extending the
Blessings of Love

Loving the Poor

Who are the poorest of the poor? They are the unwanted, the unloved, the ignored, the hungry, the naked, the homeless, the leper, and the alcoholic in our midst....To be able to see and love Jesus in the poor, we must be one with Christ through a life of deep prayer.

Jesus is reliving His passion in our poor people. The poor are really going through the passion of Christ. We should treat them with dignity....Give to Christ in His distressing disguise. It is Jesus in the poor that you feed, clothe, and take in. Do it all with a great, undivided love.

*T*he poor do not need our compassion or our pity; they need our help.

We need the eyes of deep faith to see Christ in the broken body and dirty clothes under which the Most Beautiful One among the sons of men hides.

*T*he poor are very lovable people, who give us more, much more, than we give them. We must know them. Knowledge will lead us to love; love will lead us to service.

It is not so bad to have at least one congregation that spoils the poor, when everybody else spoils the rich. I am deeply impressed by the fact that before explaining the word of God, before presenting to the crowds the Eight Beatitudes, Jesus had compassion on them and gave them food. Only then did He begin to teach them.

*T*he poor are wonderful people. They have their own dignity, which we can easily see....But the poor have, above all, great courage to lead the life they lead. They are forced to live like that; poverty has been imposed on them.

N ever turn your back on the poor, for if you do so, you are turning your back on Christ Jesus.

Not even in the early times did I ever ask for money. I wanted to serve the poor exclusively out of love for God. I wanted the poor to receive freely what the rich get with money.

Loving Our Own

Do we know the poor in our house, in our family? Perhaps they are not hungry for a piece of bread. Perhaps our children, husband, wife, are not hungry, or naked, or dispossessed, but are you sure there is no one there who feels unwanted, deprived of affection? Where is your elderly father or mother?

Intense love does not measure. . . it just gives.

One day at a meeting...I told the people, "Husbands, smile at your wives; wives, smile at your husbands." They could not understand how I was able to tell them this sort of thing. One of them asked me, "Are you married?" I said, "Yes, and sometimes I find it very difficult to smile at Jesus because He can be so demanding."

May you make of your homes another Nazareth. May Jesus be able to come and rest, to bring peace, love, and joy to your hearts and to your homes.

*I*n our day we see with growing clarity that the sorrows of the world have their origin in the family. We do not have time to look at each other, to exchange a greeting, to share a moment of joy. We take still less time to be what our children expect of us, what our spouse expects of us. And thus, each day we belong less and less to our own homes.

Thoughtfulness is the beginning of great sanctity. If you learn this art of being thoughtful, you will become more and more Christlike, for His heart was meek and He always thought of others. Jesus "went about doing good."

Maybe in our own family we have somebody who is feeling lonely, who is feeling sick, who is feeling worried, and these are difficult days for everybody. Are we there? Are we there to receive them?

*D*o not be surprised or become preoccupied at each other's failure; rather see and find in each other good, for each one of us is created in the image of God.

*I*n one word, be a real branch on the vine, Jesus. The surest means to this will be to deepen our love for each other; knowing each other's lovableness; feeling the need of each other; speaking well of each other and to each other; appreciating and knowing each other's gifts and abilities.

Loving Others

We will never know how much good just a simple smile can do. We tell people how kind, forgiving, and understanding God is—are we the living proof? Can they really see this kindness, this forgiveness, this understanding, alive in us?

W hen you look at the inner workings of electrical things, often you see small and big wires, new and old, cheap and expensive line up. Until the current passes through them there will be no light. That wire is you and me. The current is God. We have the power to let the current pass through us, use us, produce the light of the world—Jesus. Or we can refuse to be used and allow darkness to spread.

*T*hose who are unwanted and unloved...those who walk through the world with no one to care for them. Do we go out to meet those? Do we know them? Do we try to find them?

*Kindness has converted
more people than zeal, science,
or eloquence.*

I never think in terms of crowds in general, but in terms of persons. Were I to think about crowds, I would never begin anything. It is the person that matters. I believe in person-to-person encounters.

Love has a hem to her garment,
that reaches the very dust.
It sweeps the stains
from the streets and lanes,
And because it can, it must.

*T*o be true, love has to hurt....Jesus said, "Love one another as I have loved you." He loved until it hurt.

I find it is not difficult to give a plate of rice to a hungry person, to furnish a bed to a person who has no bed, but to console or to remove that bitterness, to remove that anger, to remove that loneliness, takes a long time.

Loving must be as normal to us
as living and breathing,
day after day until our death.

Our works of charity are nothing but the overflow of our love of God from within. Therefore, the one who is most united to Him loves her neighbor most.

*I*f sometimes we feel as if the Master is away, is it not because I have kept myself far from some [sister or brother]?

Serving

The very fact that God has placed a certain soul in your way is a sign that God wants to do something for her.

You need only ask at night before you go to bed, "What did I do *to* Jesus today? What did I do *for* Jesus today? What did I do *with* Jesus today?" You have only to look at your hands. This is the best examination of conscience.

I think the person who is attached to riches, who lives with the worry of riches, is actually very poor. If this person puts his money at the service of others, then he is very, very rich.

*T*he devil is very busy. The more our work involves bringing souls to God, the more he tries to take us away from God, to spoil the work.

We deliberately renounce all desires to see the fruit of our labor, doing all we can as best we can, leaving the rest in the hands of God.

C hrist's life was not written while He was living, even though He accomplished the most important work that exists: redeeming the world and teaching mankind to love His Father. Our work is Christ's work, and so we have to be His instruments, to carry out our small task and to disappear.

Giving

One thing I ask of you: never be afraid of giving, but do not give your surplus. Give to a point that it is difficult for you.

We may not be able to give much, but we can always give the joy that springs from a heart that is in love with God.

*Jesus wants us to
give of ourselves
every moment.*

May God give back to you in love all the love you have given, and all the joy and peace you have sown around you.

*H*ow has Jesus loved us? By giving Himself to us. This is how we are to love each other: by giving ourselves to each other, giving ourselves to the point of feeling pain.

Becoming a
Blessing of Love

Holiness

The first step toward holiness is the will to attain it. With a will that is whole we love God, we opt for Him, we run toward Him, we reach Him, we possess Him.

*I*f you are humble, nothing will touch you, neither praise nor disgrace, because you know what you are....If you are a saint, thank God. If you are a sinner, do not remain so.

Our eyes are like two windows through which Christ or the world comes to our hearts. Often we need great courage to keep them closed. How often we say, "I wish I had not seen this thing," and yet we take so little trouble to overcome the desire to see everything.

When one comes in touch with money, one loses contact with God....One day there springs up the desire for money and for all that money can provide—the superfluous, luxury in eating, luxury in dressing, trifles. Needs increase because one thing calls for another. The result is uncontrollable dissatisfaction.

*I*t is much easier to conquer a country than to conquer ourselves. Every act of disobedience weakens the spiritual life. It is like a wound letting out every drop of one's blood.

We cannot decide to become saints without a great effort of renunciation, of resisting temptations, of combat, of persecution, and of all sorts of sacrifices. It is not possible to love God except at one's own expense.

Pride destroys everything.

*Holiness grows fast
where there is kindness.*

All of our words will be useless unless they come from the bottom of our hearts. Words which do not spread the light of Christ increase the darkness.

*T*emptation is like fire in which gold is purified. So we have to go through this fire. The temptations are allowed by God. The only thing we have to do is refuse to give in....We have to fight temptation for the love of God.

*C*hrist tells us to aim very high, not to be like Abraham or David or any of the saints, but to be like our heavenly Father.

*Holiness is to take whatever
Jesus gives us and to give Jesus whatever
He asks of us with a big smile.*

Trust

We must never get into the habit of being preoccupied with the future. There is no reason to do so. God is there.

One thing Jesus asks of me: that I lean on Him; that in Him and only in Him I put complete trust; that I surrender myself to Him unreservedly....Even if we feel like a boat without a compass on the high seas, we are to commit ourselves fully to Him, without trying to control His actions.

*I*t must have been so hard to have been scourged, to have been spat upon. "Take it away," Jesus prayed during His agony. His Father didn't come to Him directly and say, "This is my beloved Son," but He consoled Him through an angel. Let us pray that we will fill our hearts with Jesus' surrender, that we will understand total surrender.

*D*o not give in to discouragement....If you are discouraged it is a sign of pride because it shows you trust in your own powers. Never bother about people's opinions. Be humble, and you will never be disturbed.

In the time of the Old Testament God was known as the God of fear, punishment, and anger. The coming of Jesus reverses this picture completely. God in the New Testament is the God of love, compassion, and mercy. That is why we can trust Him fully—there is no more fear.

*T*otal abandonment consists of giving oneself fully to God because God has given Himself to us. If God, who owes us nothing, is willing to give us nothing less than Himself, can we respond by giving only part of ourselves? Renouncing myself, I give myself to God so that He might live in me.

Joy

"That my joy may be in you," says Jesus. What is this joy of Jesus? It is the result of His continual union with God, doing the will of the Father. This joy is the fruit of union with God, of being in the presence of God.

When you go out for your task, spread all around you the joy of belonging to God, of living with God, of being His own.

What would our life be like if the sisters were not cheerful? It would be mere slavery. We would work without attracting anybody.

*J*oy must be one of the pivots of our life. It is the token of a generous personality. Sometimes it is also a mantle that clothes a life of sacrifice and self-giving.

I am accustomed to seeing smiling faces. I think a smile generates a smile, just as love generates love.

*J*oy is one of the best safeguards against temptation. The devil is a carrier of dust and dirt; he uses every chance to throw what he has at us. A joyful heart knows how to protect herself from such dirt. Jesus can take full possession of our soul only if it surrenders itself joyfully.

*H*oly souls sometimes undergo great inward trial, and they know darkness. But if we want others to become aware of the presence of Jesus, we must be the first ones convinced of it.

A joyful heart
is the normal result of
a heart burning with love.

Prayer

We should be professionals in prayer.

*L*ove to pray, feel the need to pray often during the day, and take the trouble to pray.

If you want to pray better, you must pray more.

God speaks in the silence of our heart, and we listen. And then we speak to God from the fullness of our heart, and God listens. And this listening and this speaking is what prayer is meant to be: that oneness with God, that oneness with Jesus.

*S*ouls of prayer are souls of deep silence. We cannot place ourselves directly in the presence of God without forcing ourselves to an inner and an outer silence. Therefore, we have to get used to the silence of the spirit, of the eyes, and of the tongue.

*Often a deep fervent
look at Christ may make
the most fervent prayer.*

P ray lovingly like children, with an earnest desire to love much and to make loved the one that is not loved.

We have to pray on behalf of those who do not pray.

The value of our actions
corresponds exactly to the value
of the prayer we make.

Prayer enlarges the heart until
it is capable of containing
God's gift of Himself.

*J*esus always waits for us in silence. In silence He listens to us; in silence He speaks to our souls. In silence we are granted the privilege of listening to His voice.

Living and Dying

We must not be afraid to proclaim Christ's love and to love as He loved. In the work we do—it does not matter how small and humble it may be—make it Christ's love in action.

*S*uffering, pain, sorrow, humiliation, feelings of loneliness, are nothing but a sign that you have come so close to Jesus that He can kiss you.

*D*eath, in the final analysis, is only the easiest and quickest means to go back to God. If only we could make people understand that we come from God and that we have to go back to Him! Going back to Him is going back home.